STARS

A TRUE BOOK

by
Paul P. Sipiera

Children's Press®
A Division of Grolier Publishing
New York London Hong Kong Sydney
Danbury, Connecticut

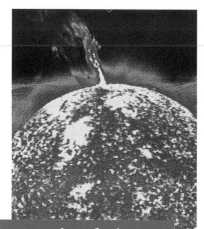

A photograph of the Sun taken by a special telescope

Reading Consultant
Linda Cornwell
Learning Resource Consultant
Indiana Department of Education

Science Consultant
Samuel Storch
Lecturer,
American Museum-Hayden Planetarium, New York City

Dedicated to the memory of astronaut Karl G. Henize, an astronomer who made it to the stars!

Library of Congress Cataloging-in-Publication Data

Sipiera, Paul P.
    Stars / by Paul Sipiera.
        p.   cm. — (A true book)
    Includes bibliographical references and index.
    Summary: Explains the nature, formation, and death of stars.
    ISBN 0-516-20341-X (lib.bdg.)   0-516-26177-0 (pbk.)
    1. Stars—Juvenile literature. [1. Stars.] I. Title. II. Series.
QB801.7.S62 1997
523.8—dc20   96-36150
                                                              CIP
                                                              AC

Contents

The Milky Way as seen from
Mount Rainier National Park
in Washington State

Starry Nights

Ancient astronomers knew the sky well. By day, they watched the bright Sun cross the sky. Sometimes they even saw the Moon during day-light. At night, little points of light called stars would appear. Early in the evening, only the brightest stars could

5

be seen. Later, as the sky darkened, hundreds more would fill the heavens. There was even a mysterious band of light that could be followed through the sky. This was called the Milky Way.

Each night, most of the stars seemed to move from east to west. They would rise and then set. A few stars were different. These seemed to circle around a star that never moved. It was called the North Star.

The North Star, which is the last star in the handle of the Little Dipper

People began to remember the brightest stars. In time, they named these stars after important people or events. By connecting the brightest

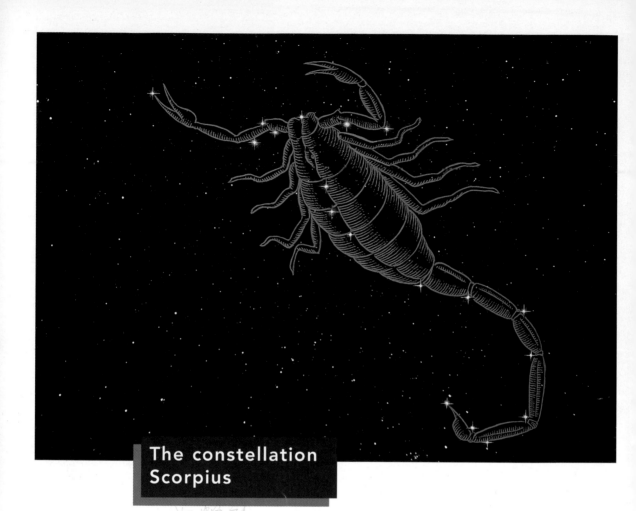

The constellation
Scorpius

stars, they made shapes or
patterns of familiar things.
These were later called
constellations.

A Use for Stars

Over time, people noticed that different stars and constellations could be seen in each season. People could predict seasonal changes by watching for certain stars to appear. This is how the first calendars were made. Later, when people began to make

An ancient Greek astronomer

great journeys, they used the stars to help them find their way home.

The ancient Greek people were expert sailors. They sailed

all over the Mediterranean Sea and out into the Atlantic Ocean. Their knowledge of the stars helped them find their way from port to port. The Cheyenne Indians of North America used the rising point of special stars to guide them across the Great Plains.

Different people from all over the world used stars for different things. Many cultures worshiped the stars as gods. In the stars, they saw their gods watching over them.

In time of need, people would pray to the stars for help.

Although ancient people knew how to use the stars, they knew little about them. What are stars? How far away are they? Who made the stars? These were some of the questions people asked.

Often, people explained the stars through stories of their gods and heroes. To many people, the heavens were a sacred and mysterious place.

Questions about the stars could not be answered until recent times. Ancient astronomers thought that all

Before the 1600s, many people thought the stars where attached to a glass sphere that moved around the Earth.

stars were attached to a glass sphere that moved around the Earth.

In 1609, Italian astronomer Galileo started to answer all the questions about stars when he looked at the sky with a new instrument called the telescope. With the telescope, he realized that the stars were very far away, and that there were too many to count.

An illustration of Galileo showing a visitor how his telescope works

What Is a Star?

A star is a huge amount of gas held in the shape of a ball by the force of gravity. The center of a star is extemely hot. The star gives off a lot of energy. This energy is produced by a process called nuclear fusion. Fusion occurs when four atoms of hydrogen

are changed into one atom of helium and a lot of energy.

Our Sun is a star. The light and heat we receive from the Sun come from this fusion process. Light and heat are what make a star different

Our Sun (left) is the nearest star to Earth. Stars, such as the Sun (bottom), produce their own light and heat.

from a planet. Stars make
their own light and heat.
Planets only reflect the light
from the star they orbit.

Stars come in many different sizes. There are giants
and there are dwarfs. The
size of a star depends upon

how much matter it contains. This is called a star's mass. For most of their lives, stars that have a large mass are usually big and bright. Those with a small mass are small and dim. Our Sun is just about average.

The color of a star's light can tell astronomers certain things. Stars that give off red light are the cooler ones. Blue stars are the really hot ones. Look at a fire in a fireplace. When the fire is burning

The hottest stars give off blue light. Stars that give off reddish light are older, cooler stars.

brightly, you will see white and blue flames. When the wood has burned down to coals, only the red glow is left. When stars are young, they burn fast and hot. As they get older, they burn more slowly and at cooler temperatures.

How bright a star appears to us depends not on its temperature, but on its size. The biggest stars usually appear to be the brightest. Small stars look dim.

The apparent brightness of a star depends also on its distance from us. Our Sun is an average-sized star. In our sky, it is the brightest star. That is because it is close to us, only 93 million miles (150 million kilometers) away. If our

Sun were as far away as the next nearest star, Alpha Centauri (26 trillion miles/42 trillion km), it would appear to be only a faint star to us.

Where Are the Stars?

All of the stars you see at night belong to the Milky Way galaxy. A galaxy is a large collection of stars that move around a common center of gravity. There are more than 200 billion stars in the Milky Way alone. Many of these stars are like the Sun. It is believed that many of them may have planets orbiting them.

The Milky
Way, as
seen from
Australia

Beyond the Milky Way galaxy
are billions of other galaxies.
They come in many different
sizes and shapes. Each has
billions of stars. Within these
galaxies, stars are being born
and are dying all the time.

The galaxy above, called M101, is a spiral galaxy. The Milky Way is a spiral galaxy as well. The galaxy at right is known as the Cartwheel galaxy.

In our Milky Way, the older stars are found near the center of the galaxy. Most of them are red or orange. The younger stars, which are blue, yellow, and white, are out in the spiral arms of the galaxy. This is where the largest amounts of gas and dust are located.

This is an artist's impression of a sideways view of the Milky Way. It shows how the older stars are in the center of the galaxy, while the younger ones are out on the spiral arms.

The Sun

Since stars are so very far from Earth, it is hard for astronomers to study them. Even in the largest telescopes, stars always appear as tiny points of light.

To better understand stars, astronomers look to the nearest star, the Sun. Of course, you should never look

SIZE OF EARTH

This photograph of the Sun was taken with a special telescope. The white dot in the top left corner shows how big the Earth is in comparison to the Sun.

at the Sun with an ordinary telescope, or even with a pair of binoculars. You might permanently damage your eyes. Astronomers can view the Sun through special

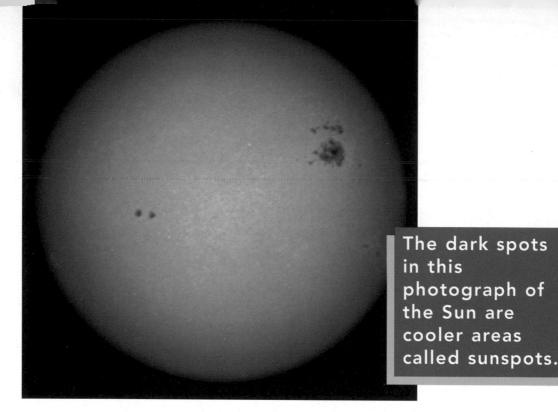

The dark spots in this photograph of the Sun are cooler areas called sunspots.

telescopes equipped with filters that block out most of the Sun's light.

Using these telescopes on Earth and in space, astronomers can see the Sun's surface features in detail. They

Solar Flares

As this false-color image of the Sun shows, stars have sudden outbursts of energy and matter from their surface. The smaller outbursts are called flares. The larger ones are called prominences. When solar flares reach the Earth's atmosphere, they can cause northern lights displays.

A northern lights display in Alaska

count the number of sunspots and measure the length of flares. These observations help scientists understand how the Sun affects the Earth.

By studying other stars, astronomers can also learn much about the Sun. They can see what the Sun must have been like billions of years ago, and what it may be like in the future. Whatever happens to the Sun will certainly affect life on Earth.

Life and Death of Stars

Stars, like people, have a birth, life, and death. Every star begins its life in a large gas-and-dust cloud called a nebula. Here, atoms are pulled together by the force of gravity. As more and more matter comes together, a

A star begins its life as a large cloud of gas and dust called a nebula (above left). As nuclear fusion occurs (above right), the new star blazes bright. After the star settles down (right), it gives off a steady amount of heat and light. This stage in a star's life usually lasts billions of years.

dark sphere forms. At its center, the temperature rises. As the sphere contracts, it gets hotter. Finally, it becomes a glowing ball of gas.

If a forming star has enough mass, nuclear fusion will begin, and the star begins to shine. At first, the star blazes brightly, but it soon settles down to give off a steady amount of heat and light. This will last for billions of years.

Near the end of a star's life, it becomes much larger and

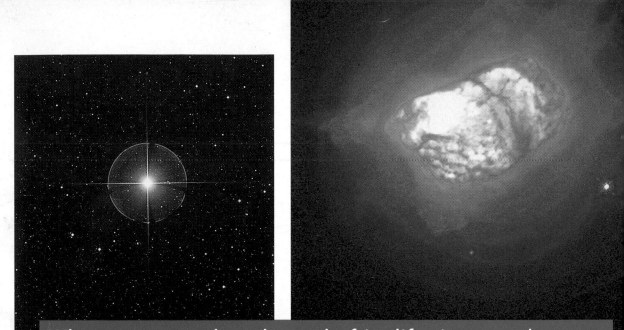

When a star reaches the end of its life, it expands to more than 50 times its original diameter, becoming a red giant star. This red supergiant (left) is the star Antares. On the right is a photograph of a dying star. It shows how the outer layers of the red giant are ejected into space, exposing the small, extremely hot core of the star, which cools off to become a white dwarf.

cooler. The star becomes a red giant. After that, many stars become white dwarf stars and then die out.

A Star "Nursery"

Would you like to see a "nursery" of stars? In winter, look for the constellation of Orion the Hunter. Find the three stars in his belt. Below the middle star, you will see a fuzzy patch of light. This is the Great Nebula in Orion. Here, hundreds of stars are forming.

This is a supernova called SN1987A. The rings surrounding it are gas being expelled from the exploding nebula.

Not all stars have such predictable lives. Super giant stars have short and very explosive lives. They begin their lives as big, hot stars that quickly run through their fuel. At their death, they give off energy so fast that they explode. This is called a supernova. A supernova can be the most powerful event in a galaxy. If a supernova exploded close to Earth, it would surely destroy all life on our planet.

One of the strangest objects in the universe is a black hole. Black holes are believed to form after a supernova has destroyed a giant star. What remains after the explosion creates the strongest force imaginable. This force of gravity is so strong that it even pulls light into it. Black holes are so mysterious that astronomers are not sure what happens inside of them.

Our Cosmic Connection

The life-and-death cycles of stars have created most of the chemical elements found on Earth. The iron in our blood and the calcium in our bones were once made inside stars.

The death of a star spews material into space. That

material can form parts of another nebula that can form into new stars. So, the death of a star leads to the birth of another, and any planets that may orbit it. In that way, we all share in the life of a star. Rocks, plants, and people are all made from the same elements formed so long ago. We are all children of the stars!

A supernova (the small green spot at upper left) in the spiral galaxy M51

To Find Out More

Here are some additional resources to help you learn more about stars:

 **Books**

 **Organizations**

Asimov, Isaac, **Library of the Universe: Projects in Astronomy**. Gareth Stevens, Inc. 1990.

Dolan, Terrance, **Probing Deep Space.** Chelsea House. 1993.

Muirden, James, **Stars and Planets.** Grolier. 1994.

Simon, Seymour, **Stars.** Morrow & Company, Inc. 1986

Sipiera, Paul P., **Black Holes.** Children's Press. 1997

Astronomical Society of the Pacific
1290 24th Avenue
San Francisco, CA 94122
http://www.physics.sfsu. edu/asp

The Planetary Society
65 North Catalina Avenue
Pasadena, CA 91106
e-mail: *tps.lc@genie.geis.com*

The Royal Astronomical Society of Canada

La Societe Royala d'Astronomie du Canada
136 Dupont Street,
Toronto, Ontario
Canada M5R 1V2

Online Sites

Astronet
*http://www.xs4all.nl/~
carlkop/astroeng.html*

**Astronomy—What's Up
This Month**
*http:/www1.tmlsnet.com/~
abdale/Astronomy/
Astronomy.html*

**Constellations and
Their Stars**
*http://www.astro.wisc.edu/
~dolan/constellations*

**The Planetary Studies
Foundation**
*http://homepage.
interaccess.com/~jpatpsf/>.*

Sky Online
http:/www.skypub.com/

Important Words

astronomer scientist who studies the stars, planets, and other heavenly bodies

atom the smallest unit of a chemical element

chemical element one of the 92 materials that make up all things in nature; these include hydrogen, carbon, oxygen, helium, sodium, silver, gold, and others

matter all things that exist as a gas, liquid, or solid

nuclear fusion a process in which two or more elements are combined to form a new element; when this happens, a large amount of energy is released

nucleus the center part of an object

solar wind a gaslike substance constantly being thrown off by the Sun into space

supernova a huge explosion that destroys a giant star; during the explosion, the star gives off as much energy as an entire galaxy

Index

Meet the Author

Paul P. Sipiera is a professor of geology and astronomy at William Rainey Harper College in Palatine, Illinois. His main area of research is meteorites. When he is not studying science, he can be found working on his farm in Galena, Illinois, with his wife, Diane, and their three daughters, Andrea, Paula Frances, and Carrie Ann.